W9-DFU-906

TEAM SPIRIT®

SMART BOOKS FOR YOUNG FANS

THE SEATTLE SEAHAWKS

BY
MARK STEWART

New Hanover County Public Library
201 Chestnut Street
Wilmington, North Carolina 28401

NORWOOD HOUSE PRESS

CHICAGO, ILLINOIS

Norwood House Press
P.O. Box 316598
Chicago, Illinois 60631

For information regarding Norwood House Press, please visit our website at:
www.norwoodhousepress.com or call 866-565-2900.

All photos courtesy of Getty Images except the following:
SportsChrome (4), Seattle Seahawks/NFL (7, 21, 31, 33, 36),
Topps, Inc. (9, 11, 15, 20, 28, 34 both, 37, 38, 40, 43 top right, 45),
Icon SMI (14), Black Book Partners (16, 24, 35 top right, 38, 43 bottom right), Matt Richman (48).
Cover Photo: Icon SMI

The memorabilia and artifacts pictured in this book are presented for educational and informational purposes,
and come from the collection of the author.

Editor: Mike Kennedy
Designer: Ron Jaffe
Project Management: Black Book Partners, LLC.
Special thanks to Topps, Inc.

Library of Congress Cataloging-in-Publication Data

Stewart, Mark, 1960-
    The Seattle Seahawks / by Mark Stewart.
        p. cm. -- (Team spirit)
    Includes bibliographical references and index.
    Summary: "A revised Team Spirit Football edition featuring the Seattle
Seahawks that chronicles the history and accomplishments of the team.
Includes access to the Team Spirit website which provides additional
information and photos"--Provided by publisher.
    ISBN 978-1-59953-539-5 (library edition : alk. paper) -- ISBN
978-1-60357-481-5 (ebook) 1. Seattle Seahawks (Football
team)--History--Juvenile literature. I. Title.
    GV956.S4S84 2012
    796.332'6409797772--dc23
                                                        2012020038

Manufactured in the United States of America in North Mankato, Minnesota.
270R—112014

COVER PHOTO: The Seahawks prepare to make a defensive stand.

Table of Contents

ABOUT OUR GLOSSARY

In this book, there may be several words that you are reading for the first time. Some are sports words, some are new vocabulary words, and some are familiar words that are used in an unusual way. All of these words are defined on page 46. Throughout the book, sports words appear in **bold type**. Regular vocabulary words appear in ***bold italic type***.

A seahawk is a powerful, quick, and clever bird. Football fans in Washington know all about those qualities. When the Seattle Seahawks take the field, they win with strength, speed, and intelligence.

The Seahawks have had many great players over the years, but they are not a team of superstars. Everyone on the roster—from the starters to the **role players**—works equally hard to prepare for each game. When the Seahawks win, they win as a team. When they lose, they learn lessons that make the team better.

This book tells the story of the Seahawks. Sports fans in Seattle are among the best in the nation. They support the team through thick and thin, and they cheer for plays that people in other cities might not notice. The Seahawks love this about their fans. That's why they give everything they've got every time they take the field.

The Seahawks' defense keeps an eye on the clock. They are ready for every game situation.

Glory Days

During the 1940s and 1950s, the population of Seattle grew very quickly. During the 1960s and 1970s, the city became a center for people of different *cultures* and a place for *international* business. The people of Seattle were proud of the progress they had made. The only thing missing was a team in the **National Football League (NFL)**.

In 1972, the city began construction on a new stadium called the Kingdome. Two years later, the NFL awarded Seattle one of two new teams for the 1976 season. The Seahawks got to work on building their roster. They selected unwanted players from other NFL teams, discovered college stars in the **draft**, and also held tryouts. Seattle's main goal was to find a good quarterback who could lead the team. The man who won the job rolled into town in a broken-down Volkswagen Beetle.

His name was Jim Zorn, and he had a strong left arm and quick feet. He would need them with the Seahawks. In Seattle's early years, Zorn often found himself scrambling away from defenders. His favorite target was Steve Largent, a small receiver with good hands and great **determination**. He would go on to be the first Seahawk voted into the **Hall of Fame**.

Zorn and Largent gave Seattle a dangerous passing attack. Running back Sherman Smith rounded out the offense. The defense, however, was another matter. The Seahawks allowed more than 30 points a game in their first season and finished with a record of 2–12.

Over the next few seasons, Seattle's defense improved, and the team began to show signs that it could be a championship **contender**. In the 1980s, the Seahawks added three new stars: safety Kenny Easley, pass-rusher Jacob Green, and running back

LEFT: Jim Zorn and Steve Largent
ABOVE: Kenny Easley

Curt Warner. They also replaced Zorn with Dave Krieg. In 1983, Krieg led the Seahawks to the championship game of the **American Football Conference (AFC)**. Five years later, Seattle won the **AFC West** for the first time. By then, Brian Blades and John L. Williams had joined the team to give the offense an extra boost.

The Seahawks had many good players in the 1990s, including Cortez Kennedy, Eugene Robinson, Joey Galloway, Michael Sinclair, Chris Warren, Ricky Watters, and Warren Moon. Unfortunately, they struggled to win games. In 1999, Seattle hired coach Mike Holmgren. He had led the Green Bay Packers to the **Super Bowl** twice.

The Seahawks won the AFC West in Holmgren's first season. The team enjoyed even more success after moving to the **National Football Conference (NFC)** in 2002. Seattle finished first in the **NFC West** in 2004. Running back Shaun Alexander and quarterback Matt Hasselbeck led the offense. Both players were known for their talent and toughness. They benefitted from a

LEFT: Shaun Alexander looks for a hole in the defense.
ABOVE: This trading card shows Matt Hasselbeck in action.

powerful offensive line that included Walter Jones, Robbie Tobeck, and Steve Hutchinson. Alexander became the league's top rusher. Hasselbeck *inspired* his teammates with his desire to win.

The 2005 season was even better. Alexander set an NFL record with 28 touchdowns. Hasselbeck threw for 3,459 yards and 24 touchdowns. Fullback Mack Strong was named **All-Pro**. The leader of the defense was Lofa Tatupu. He got plenty of help from Jordan Babineaux, Michael Boulware, and Rocky Bernard. Seattle went 13–3 in the regular season and rolled into the **playoffs**. With their fans cheering them on, they won their first NFC championship and played in the Super Bowl for the first time.

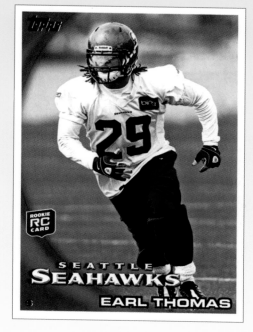

In the years that followed, age and injuries slowed down the Seahawks. The team began rebuilding around a new group of stars that included Earl Thomas, Matt Flynn, Bruce Irvin, and Marshawn Lynch. Seattle also hired Pete Carroll to lead the team from the sidelines. He had been a great college coach. Carroll brought new *enthusiasm* to the Seahawks.

Seattle fans watched carefully to see how well these "puzzle pieces" fit into place. In 2010, the Seahawks won the NFC West again and beat the mighty New Orleans Saints in the playoffs. All of Seattle celebrated the victory. The fans believed that another trip to the Super Bowl was just a matter of time.

LEFT: Leroy Hill blocks for Lofa Tatupu on an interception return.
ABOVE: This card shows Earl Thomas as a rookie in 2010.

Home Turf

The Seahawks spent their first 24 seasons in the Kingdome. They shared it with the Mariners baseball team. The Kingdome was one of the noisiest stadiums in sports. The loud crowds gave the team an extra burst of energy.

In 2002, the Seahawks opened a new stadium. They made sure the fans still had an important role to play on game day. The stadium's roof was designed to reflect crowd noise down onto the field. Much of that noise is made by fans in the "Hawk's Nest." That's a special seating section where fans can stomp on the metal bleachers to make it hard for opponents to hear each other.

BY THE NUMBERS

- The Seahawks' stadium has 72,000 seats.
- The stadium cost $360 million to build. Owner Paul Allen spent $130 million of his own money to help fund the stadium.
- Five different artists created beautiful works that are on display all over the stadium grounds.

The Seahawks and New York Giants meet on the field in Seattle.

Dressed for Success

The original colors of the Seahawks were blue and forest green. They are familiar to people in the Seattle area, where the forests often stretch down to the water's edge. Silver and white were the team's other main colors.

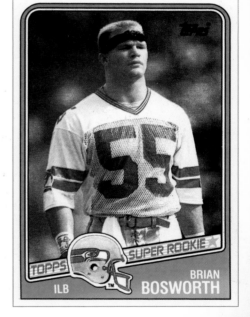

When the Seahawks moved into their new stadium in 2002, they also introduced new colors and uniforms. The team changed to darker blue, lighter green, silver-grey, and white. The Seahawks made their uniforms look more modern, too.

When it came to their helmets, the Seahawks asked their fans what they should do. The fans voted for blue helmets, instead of the old silver ones. It was the first time an NFL team let its fans decide a uniform color.

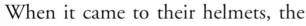

LEFT: Marshawn Lynch models Seattle's home uniform.
ABOVE: Brian Bosworth warms up in the Seahawks' road jersey from the 1980s.

We Won!

At the start of each season, the goal of each team in the NFL is to win the Super Bowl. To do that, a team must first win its conference championship. Back in 1983, when the Seahawks were still part of the AFC, they reached the conference title game for the first time. Dave Krieg and Curt Warner led the offense. Kenny Easley was the star of the defense. Seattle went 9–7 during the regular season, and then got hot in the playoffs. The Seahawks beat the Denver Broncos and followed that with a victory over the Miami Dolphins. Unfortunately, Seattle fell one win short of the AFC championship.

LEFT: Dave Krieg fires a pass. **RIGHT**: Steve Hutchinson (76) and Walter Jones (71) get ready for a play during the 2005 season.

Twenty-two years later, the Seahawks—now part of the NFC— built a team with enough talent to make it all the way to the Super Bowl. The 2005 season was just a few weeks old when football fans learned just how powerful the Seahawks were. In a game against the Arizona Cardinals, Shaun Alexander ran for 140 yards and four touchdowns. Seattle won easily, 37–12. Two weeks later, Alexander matched those numbers in a 42–10 victory over the Houston Texans.

The key for Seattle was its offensive line, which was led by Walter Jones, Steve Hutchinson, and Robbie Tobeck. They created huge holes for Alexander and Maurice Morris. Meanwhile,

Matt Hasselbeck had all the time he needed to find his receivers. The Seahawks were rolling. At one point, they won 11 games in a row.

Seattle finished the regular season with the best record in the NFC. In their first playoff game, the Seahawks hosted the Washington Redskins. Early in the contest, Alexander suffered a *concussion*. Hasselbeck and the rest of the offense picked up the slack. The Seattle quarterback threw a touchdown pass to Darrell Jackson and also ran for a score. The defense did its job by holding the Redskins to just 57 rushing yards. The Seahawks held on for a 20–10 victory.

For the first time in their history, the Seahawks were going to the **NFC Championship Game**. The Seahawks took on the Carolina Panthers. The fans in Seattle were louder than they had ever been. The Panthers never had a chance.

Seattle struck first on a touchdown pass from Hasselbeck to tight end Jerramy Stevens. Kicker Josh Brown followed that score a few minutes later with a short **field goal**. Next it was Alexander's turn. Back from his head injury, he plunged into the end zone from the 1-yard line for a touchdown. The Seahawks led 17–0.

In the second half, Seattle continued to pour it on. Jackson caught a touchdown pass from Hasselbeck. Alexander scored his second touchdown of the game. The defense, meanwhile, gave the Panthers little room to move. The Seahawks **intercepted** three passes and **sacked** Carolina's quarterback twice.

Seattle cruised to a 34–14 victory. The fans celebrated long into the night. In their 30th season, the Seahawks had finally reached the Super Bowl!

LEFT: Matt Hasselbeck celebrates his touchdown run.
ABOVE: Shaun Alexander shows the crowd the NFC championship trophy.

To be a true star in the NFL, you need more than fast feet and a big body. You have to be a "go-to guy"—someone the coach wants on the field at the end of a big game. Seahawks fans have had a lot to cheer about over the years, including these great stars …

THE PIONEERS

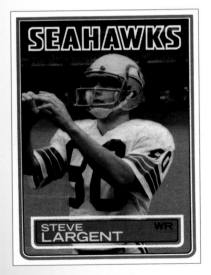

STEVE LARGENT — Receiver

• BORN: 9/28/1954 • PLAYED FOR TEAM: 1976 TO 1989

No one ran more precise pass routes or had better hands than Steve Largent. He set a record by catching a pass in 177 games in a row. Largent retired as Seattle's all-time leader in receptions, receiving yards, and receiving touchdowns.

JIM ZORN — Quarterback

• BORN: 5/10/1953 • PLAYED FOR TEAM: 1976 TO 1984

Jim Zorn was a fan favorite in Seattle. He was a good leader who could make a big play at any time. Zorn guided the Seahawks to their first two winning seasons, in 1978 and 1979.

DAVE KRIEG

Quarterback

• BORN: 10/20/1958 • PLAYED FOR TEAM: 1980 TO 1991

Dave Krieg waited more than three years to get the chance to be Seattle's starting quarterback. He made the most of the opportunity. In 1984, Krieg threw 32 touchdown passes, led the team to the playoffs, and was selected to play in the **Pro Bowl**.

JACOB GREEN

Defensive Lineman

• BORN: 1/21/1957 • PLAYED FOR TEAM: 1980 TO 1992

Jacob Green was a dangerous pass-rusher. He had more than 100 sacks for the Seahawks. Green also returned two interceptions for scores.

KENNY EASLEY

Defensive Back

• BORN: 1/15/1959 • PLAYED FOR TEAM: 1981 TO 1987

Kenny Easley was tall, fast, and powerful. He glided around the field to make tackles and interceptions. Easley was the best safety in the NFL until an injury ended his career at the age of 28.

JOHN L. WILLIAMS

Running Back

• BORN: 11/23/1964 • PLAYED FOR TEAM: 1986 TO 1993

Fullback John L. Williams was a great blocker who surprised opponents with his ability to run with the ball and catch passes. He did whatever the Seahawks asked of him. Williams made the Pro Bowl in 1990 and 1991.

LEFT: Steve Largent
ABOVE: Jacob Green

CORTEZ KENNEDY   Defensive Lineman

• BORN: 8/23/1968   • PLAYED FOR TEAM: 1990 TO 2000

Cortez Kennedy was a huge lineman with great quickness. He teamed up with Sam Adams to make running up the middle against the Seahawks almost impossible. Kennedy was the 1992 Defensive Player of the Year.

MACK STRONG   Running Back

• BORN: 9/1//1971   • PLAYED FOR TEAM: 1994 TO 2007

Mack Strong took over at fullback from John L. Williams, and the Seahawks kept rolling. Strong blocked for Shaun Alexander during his five 1,000-yard seasons. He was honored as an All-Pro in 2005.

WALTER JONES   Offensive Lineman

• BORN: 1/19/1974   • PLAYED FOR TEAM: 1997 TO 2009

Walter Jones was a tower of power on the offensive line. He could open huge holes on running plays and keep Seattle's quarterbacks safe on passing plays. Jones played in nine Pro Bowls as a Seahawk.

SHAUN ALEXANDER   Running Back

• BORN: 8/30/1977   • PLAYED FOR TEAM: 2000 TO 2007

For five years starting in 2001, Shaun Alexander was the best running back in the NFL. Few players have ever been as good near the goal line. Alexander led the NFC in touchdowns four times and was the NFL **Most Valuable Player (MVP)** in 2005.

MATT HASSELBECK   Quarterback

- BORN: 9/25/1975   • PLAYED FOR TEAM: 2001 TO 2007

Matt Hasselbeck became the team's starting
quarterback in 2001. Four years later, the
Seahawks won their first conference championship.
Hasselbeck was a tough *competitor* who never
gave up on a game.

LOFA TATUPU   Linebacker

- BORN: 11/15/1982   • PLAYED FOR TEAM: 2005 TO 2010

Lofa Tatupu was smaller than most linebackers,
but he used his tremendous speed to become
one of the league's best defenders. Tatupu always
seemed to be around the ball. In six seasons, he
had 10 interceptions, caused seven **fumbles**, and
recovered two others.

EARL THOMAS   Defensive Back

- BORN: 5/7/1989   • FIRST YEAR WITH TEAM: 2010

Earl Thomas was a great athlete who played with tremendous passion. As
a **rookie**, he intercepted five passes. The following year, he made the Pro
Bowl. That was enough to convince the Seahawks to build their defense
around his many skills.

ABOVE: Lofa Tatupu

Calling the Shots

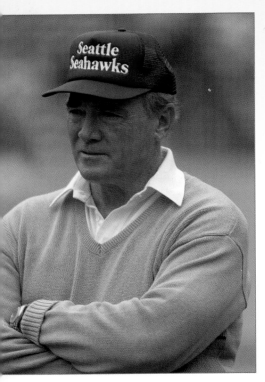

The Seahawks have always believed success starts with good coaching. Seattle's first coach was Jack Patera. During his playing days, Patera learned the game from two NFL legends, Weeb Ewbank and Tom Landry. They taught him well. With Seattle, Patera built the team into a defensive powerhouse. Thanks to his hard work, the Seahawks had a winning record in just their third year.

Chuck Knox followed Patera in 1983. Knox was famous for his love of the running game. The nickname for his offense was "Ground Chuck." Knox made an immediate impact with the Seahawks. They reached the **AFC Championship Game** in his first year. In 1988, the Seahawks won the AFC West. That made Knox—who had also coached the Los Angeles Rams and Buffalo Bills—the first person to lead three different teams to division crowns.

Mike Holmgren was the coach who guided the Seahawks to their first Super Bowl. He was hired by team owner Paul Allen in 1999. Holmgren taught his players to prepare well for games and play with great patience. Holmgren knew that keeping the score close gave the Seahawks a good chance to win games in the fourth quarter.

In 2005, the Seahawks went 13–3. Even the games they lost were close. Only one of those defeats was decided by more than a touchdown. In 10 years with Seattle, Holmgren had seven winning seasons.

In 2010, the Seahawks hired Pete Carroll to coach the team. From 2001 to 2009, Carroll was one of the most successful coaches in college football. After leading the University of Southern California to a pair of national championships, he decided it was time to jump to the NFL. The Seahawks made the playoffs in Carroll's first year.

LEFT: Chuck Knox
ABOVE: Paul Allen and Mike Holmgren

SEPTEMBER 29, 2002

No one was tougher to stop near the goal line than Shaun Alexander. The Minnesota Vikings learned this lesson the hard way in the fourth week of the 2002 season. They had high hopes heading into their game with Seattle. Alexander had gotten off to a slow start. In each of his first three games, he'd gained less than 40 yards. Seattle's record stood at 0–3.

That all changed a few minutes after kickoff. In the first quarter, Alexander smashed into the end zone on a two-yard run. Later, he scored on a 20-yard dash. The Seahawks led 17–10 with just over three minutes left in the second quarter when Alexander caught a short pass from Trent Dilfer. Alexander faked out two defenders and ran 80 yards for his third touchdown of the game. It was the longest reception of his career.

Alexander barely had a chance to catch his breath before the Seattle offense was back on the field. The Vikings fumbled the kickoff, and the

Shaun Alexander runs for a touchdown against the Minnesota Vikings.

Seahawks went back to work. Alexander took a handoff, burst through a huge hole, and ran untouched into the end zone for a touchdown.

The Seahawks kicked off again, and the Vikings fumbled again. This time, Seattle recovered the ball on the 14-yard line. Alexander jogged back on the field, and on the next play, he ran for his third touchdown in just over one minute!

Alexander's five touchdowns in the first half set an NFL record. Late in the fourth quarter, he had a chance to tie the record of six touchdowns in a game. The Seahawks had the ball on Minnesota's 5-yard line and handed off to Alexander. The Vikings finally stopped him short of the end zone. The Seahawks kicked a field goal to make the final score 48–23.

Legend Has It

Who was Seattle's best "cutback" runner?

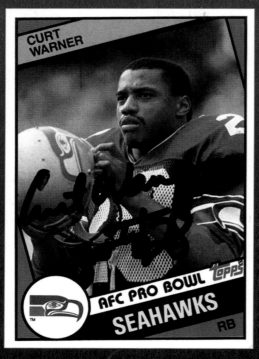

LEGEND HAS IT that Curt Warner was. A good running back is like an orchestra conductor. When he moves, everyone follows. When Warner carried the ball in one direction, opposing defenders would all start moving in the same direction to catch him. Warner loved to wait for just the right moment before he would cut back sharply in the opposite direction. By the time the defense adjusted, Warner had usually broken free for a big gain. As a rookie in 1983, he rushed for 1,449 yards. After a serious injury the following year, Warner returned in 1985 and was voted to the Pro Bowl twice.

ABOVE: Curt Warner signed this trading card, which shows his Pro Bowl accomplishment.

Did the 1998 Seahawks have the NFL's most exciting defense?

LEGEND HAS IT that they did. Eight times during the season, a Seattle player intercepted a pass and ran it back for a touchdown. Shawn Springs and Darrin Smith had two each. In a December game against the San Diego Chargers, Seattle picked off seven passes—second-most in NFL history. During the season, the Seahawks also returned two fumbles for touchdowns, and Joey Galloway and Steve Broussard brought back a total of three kicks for scores. That made 13 touchdowns produced by the defense and **special teams**. No team in history had ever scored that many.

Which Seahawk had the greatest season ever?

LEGEND HAS IT that Cortez Kennedy did. Shaun Alexander was the NFL MVP in 2005, but Kennedy had an even greater season in 1992. That year, it often took three players to block him. Even then, Kennedy found ways to stop the ball carrier. In all, he had 92 tackles and 14 sacks. When it came time to pick the NFL Defensive Player of the Year, Kennedy was the easy choice. The amazing thing is that Seattle won just twice that season—the top defensive player had never come from a team with such a poor record!

It Really Happened

As the 1979 season started, Seattle fans had high hopes for the Seahawks. The year before, the team had produced a winning record for the first time. Coach Jack Patera knew he had an excellent offense that would score lots of points. The defense, however, was another story. Patera wasn't confident that the Seahawks could keep opponents out of the end zone.

After Seattle lost five of its first seven games, Patera decided to try something new. The Seahawks would avoid punting the ball whenever possible. That meant Patera had to invent tricky fourth-down plays to keep the offense on the field. The Seahawks often tried fake punts and fake field goals. The Seattle offense became known as the "Flying Circus."

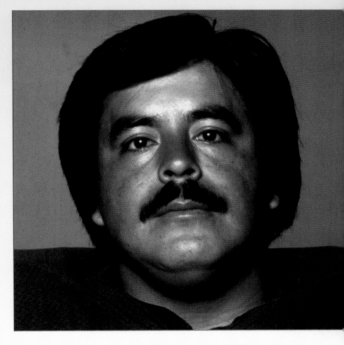

Many times during the season, with the team on the brink of disaster, Jim Zorn and Steve Largent connected on incredible pass plays. Often, it looked as if Zorn would be tackled for a big loss, but he would manage to scramble away from pass-rushers. Largent, meanwhile, never stopped trying to get open. Zorn usually found him with a pass. Largent ended up leading the NFL in receiving yards. He averaged almost 20 yards per catch.

Somehow, Patera's strategy worked. The Seahawks won seven of their final nine games to finish with a 9–7 record. In a game against the Atlanta Falcons, they won thanks to a **quarterback sneak** on fourth down, an **onside kick**, and a long pass to kicker Efren Herrera. In their next-to-last game, the Seahawks beat the Denver Broncos to knock them out of first place. The following week, they defeated the Oakland Raiders to keep them out of the playoffs. It was a season that Seattle fans are still talking about.

Team Spirit

Fans of the Seahawks know how to make noise. Seattle's stadium is one of the loudest in the league when the other team has the ball. Sometimes, Seattle fans are so noisy that the stadium feels like it's shaking.

The Seahawks know how important their fans are to the team's success. In 1984, Seattle retired jersey number 12 to honor its fans. The number 12 stands for the "12th Man"—which is a nickname that many teams use for their fans. A football team puts 11 players on the field for every play. A loud crowd is like a 12th player. Before each home game, a former player or celebrity raises a flag with the number 12 on it.

Seattle fans also get to watch a couple of hawks during home games. One is Taima, a magnificent bird that has been trained to lead the Seahawks onto the field before games. The other is Blitz, the team's big blue *mascot*.

LEFT: Even in the rain, Seattle fans love playing the role of 12th Man.
ABOVE: Chris Warren is front and center on the cover of the team's 1996 guide book.

In this timeline, each Super Bowl is listed under the year it was played. Remember that the Super Bowl is held early in the year and is actually part of the previous season. For example, Super Bowl XLVI was played on February 5, 2012, but it was the championship of the 2011 NFL season.

1978
Steve Largent is picked to play in his first Pro Bowl.

1987
Fredd Young is named All-Pro.

1976
The Seahawks play their first season.

1983
Curt Warner leads the AFC in rushing as a rookie.

1992
Cortez Kennedy is the NFL Defensive Player of the Year.

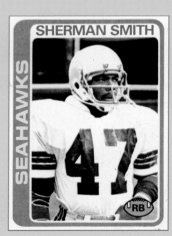

Sherman Smith was the team's top rusher in 1976.

Cortez Kennedy

Chris Warren

Michael Boulware intercepted a pass during Super Bowl XL.

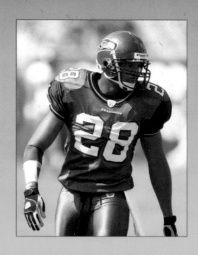

1994
Chris Warren leads the AFC in rushing.

2006
The Seahawks play in Super Bowl XL.

2012
Earl Thomas plays in the Pro Bowl.

1999
The team wins the AFC West for the second time.

2005
Shaun Alexander runs for 27 touchdowns.

2007
Patrick Kerney has 14.5 sacks.

Patrick Kerney gets a pat on the back from Lofa Tatupu.

Fun Facts

LIVE STRONG

In 1989, the Seahawks began giving out the Steve Largent Award to the player with the greatest team spirit and dedication. Running back Mack Strong won the award five times during his career. Through

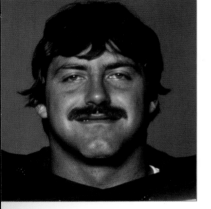

2011, no other Seahawk had won it more than once.

LEAVE IT TO BEESON

One of Seattle's early stars was linebacker Terry Beeson. He had 18 tackles in a game as a rookie in 1977. The next year he had a total of 153 tackles. Both were still team records more than 30 years later.

KICKING BACK

In 1978, his first season with the Seahawks, Efren Herrera became an instant hero when his last-second field goal beat the Oakland Raiders, 17–16. It was Seattle's second win over Oakland that year and the first time since 1965 that the Raiders had lost to the same team twice in one season.

BLOCK THAT KICK!

Defensive lineman Joe Nash was one of the most popular players on the Seahawks in the 1980s and 1990s. His specialty was blocking field goals. He batted down eight kicks during his career.

GOOD CATCH

In 2011, receiver Doug Baldwin sat through the entire draft without hearing his name called. He got a tryout with the Seahawks and made the team. In his rookie season, Baldwin was Seattle's top receiver with 51 catches and 788 yards.

NAME GAME

In 1975, Seattle's owners held a contest to choose the team's name. They received more than 20,000 entries from fans. The team decided on Seahawks, which is another name for the osprey, a bird that is native to the *Pacific Northwest*.

MR. AUTOMATIC

Norm Johnson was Seattle's kicker from 1982 to 1990. The fans nicknamed him "Mr. Automatic" because he seemed to never miss a field goal.

LEFT: Terry Beeson   **ABOVE**: Joe Nash

Talking Football

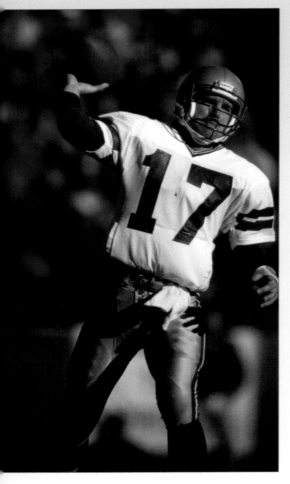

"I achieved as much as I possibly could. I always tried as hard as I could, and I worked as hard as I could."

▶ **Dave Krieg,** *on always giving his best*

"We were determined to make something of ourselves and the Seattle Seahawks."

▶ **Jim Zorn,** *on the team's attitude in its early years*

"I hope that my personal story will be an inspiration to those people who are told that they can't do something."

▶ **Steve Largent,** *on being cut by other NFL teams before joining the Seahawks*

ABOVE: Dave Krieg
RIGHT: Mike Holmgren talks to Matt Hasselbeck on the sideline.

"He is a real competitive guy. That's one of the **traits** that makes him a good player."
► *Mike Holmgren,*
on quarterback
Matt Hasselbeck

"Football is a great sport. It's an event people think about the whole week and get up for."
► *Paul Allen,* *on why*
he decided to buy
the Seahawks

"You have to be ready to come back on that next play. That's what everybody wants to see."
► *Lofa Tatupu,* *on dealing with mistakes*

"This is fifty times better than going to the Pro Bowl!"
► *Cortez Kennedy,* *on reaching the playoffs for the first time after 10 seasons*

Great Debates

People who root for the Seahawks love to compare their favorite moments, teams, and players. Some debates have been going on for years! How would you settle these classic football arguments?

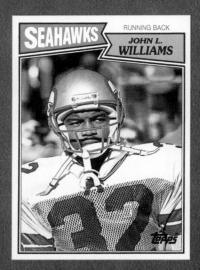

John L. Williams was the team's best fullback ...

... because he was a punishing blocker who also beat opponents as a runner and receiver. What more could you ask a fullback to do? Williams (LEFT) played eight seasons for Seattle. He gained more than 8,000 yards rushing and receiving during that time. More important, with Williams leading the charge, Curt Warner and Chris Warren combined for four 1,000-yard seasons for the Seahawks.

Mack Strong is the stronger pick here ...

... because his running mates had ten 1,000-yard seasons! Strong was one of the best blocking fullbacks in NFL history. It was like having an extra lineman in the **backfield**. Strong was also a good leader. He inspired his teammates by always working hard

Steve Largent was the all-time best Seahawk ....

… because he has the numbers to prove it. When Largent (RIGHT) retired, he had 819 catches for 13,089 yards. He wasn't just Seattle's all-time leading receiver—he was the top receiver in *professional* football history. Largent wasn't big or fast, but he had an amazing understanding of the game and caught every ball thrown his way.

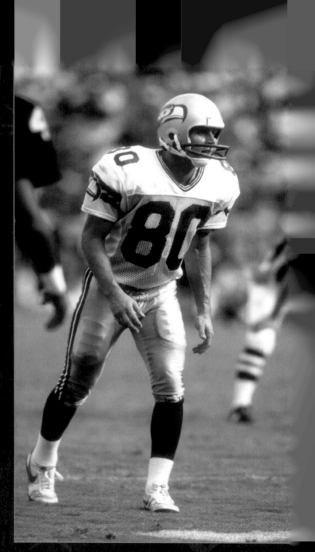

Shaun Alexander was better than Largent ....

… because for five incredible seasons, he was almost unstoppable. Alexander used his speed and power to gain more than 1,000 yards each year from 2001 to 2005. He scored 98 touchdowns during that time—an average of almost 20 per season! In 2005, Alexander was the NFL rushing champion with 1,880 yards. After the season, he was named the league MVP and Offensive Player of the Year.

The great Seahawks teams and players have left their marks on the record books. These are the "best of the best" …

Jack Patera

SEAHAWKS AWARD WINNERS

WINNER	AWARD	YEAR
Jack Patera	Coach of the Year	1978
Kenny Easley	Defensive Player of the Year	1984
Chuck Knox	Coach of the Year	1984
Cortez Kennedy	Defensive Player of the Year	1992
Shaun Alexander	Offensive Player of the Year	2005
Shaun Alexander	Most Valuable Player	2005

Shaun Alexander

SEAHAWKS ACHIEVEMENTS

ACHIEVEMENT	YEAR
AFC West Champions	1988
AFC West Champions	1999
NFC West Champions	2004
NFC West Champions	2005
NFC Champions	2005
NFC West Champions	2006
NFC West Champions	2007
NFC West Champions	2010

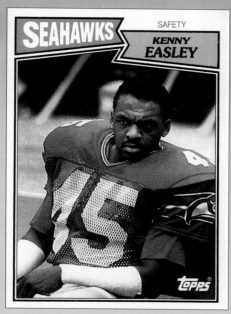

TOP RIGHT: Kenny Easley was Defensive Player of the Year in 1984.
BOTTOM RIGHT: Walter Jones starred for the NFC champions in 2005.
BELOW: Cortez Kennedy was also named Defensive Player of the Year.

Pinpoints

The history of a football team is made up of many smaller stories. These stories take place all over the map—not just in the city a team calls "home." Match the pushpins on these maps to the **Team Facts**, and you will begin to see the story of the Seahawks unfold!

TEAM FACTS

1 Seattle, Washington—*The team has played here since 1976.*

2 Oakland, California—*Marshawn Lynch was born here.*

3 Tulsa, Oklahoma—*Steve Largent was born here.*

4 Iola, Wisconsin—*Dave Krieg was born here.*

5 Orange, Texas—*Earl Thomas was born here.*

6 Wyoming, West Virginia—*Curt Warner was born here.*

7 Chesapeake, Virginia—*Kenny Easley was born here.*

8 Detroit, Michigan—*The Seahawks played in Super Bowl XL here.*

9 Osceola, Arkansas—*Cortez Kennedy was born here.*

10 Aliceville, Alabama—*Walter Jones was born here.*

11 Palatka, Florida—*John L. Williams was born here.*

12 Guadalajara, Mexico—*Efren Herrera was born here.*

Marshawn Lynch

45

Glossary

🧠 **Football Words**
🧠 **Vocabulary Words**

🧠 **AFC CHAMPIONSHIP GAME**—The game played to determine which AFC team will go to the Super Bowl.

🧠 **AFC WEST**—A division for teams that play in the western part of the country.

🧠 **ALL-PRO**—An honor given to the best players at their positions at the end of each season.

🧠 **AMERICAN FOOTBALL CONFERENCE (AFC)**—One of two groups of teams that make up the NFL.

🧠 **BACKFIELD**—The players who line up behind the line of scrimmage. On offense, the quarterback and running backs are in the backfield.

🧠 *COMPETITOR*—Someone who has a strong desire to win.

🧠 *CONCUSSION*—A head injury that affects the brain.

🧠 *CONTENDER*—A person or team that competes for a championship.

🧠 *CULTURES*—Large groups of people who share common beliefs, customs, and a way of living.

🧠 *DETERMINATION*—The desire and will to succeed.

🧠 **DRAFT**—The annual meeting during which NFL teams choose from a group of the best college players.

🧠 *ENTHUSIASM*—Strong excitement.

🧠 **FIELD GOAL**—A goal from the field, kicked over the crossbar and between the goal posts. A field goal is worth three points.

🧠 **FUMBLES**—Balls that are dropped by the players carrying them.

🧠 **HALL OF FAME**—The museum in Canton, Ohio, where football's greatest players are honored.

🧠 *INSPIRED*—Gave positive and confident feelings to others.

🧠 **INTERCEPTED**—Caught in the air by a defensive player.

🧠 *INTERNATIONAL*—From all over the world.

🧠 *MASCOT*—An animal or person believed to bring a group good luck.

🧠 **MOST VALUABLE PLAYER (MVP)**—The award given each year to the league's best player; also given to the best player in the Super Bowl and Pro Bowl.

🧠 **NATIONAL FOOTBALL CONFERENCE (NFC)**—One of two groups of teams that make up the NFL.

🧠 **NATIONAL FOOTBALL LEAGUE (NFL)**—The league that started in 1920 and is still operating today.

🧠 **NFC CHAMPIONSHIP GAME**—The game played to determine which NFC team will go to the Super Bowl.

🧠 **NFC WEST**—A division for teams that play in the western part of the country.

🧠 **ONSIDE KICK**—A short kickoff that the kicking team tries to recover.

🧠 *PACIFIC NORTHWEST*—The coastal regions of Oregon, Washington, and British Columbia, Canada.

🧠 **PLAYOFFS**—The games played after the regular season to determine which teams play in the Super Bowl.

🧠 **PRO BOWL**—The NFL's all-star game, played after the regular season.

🧠 *PROFESSIONAL*—Paid to play.

🧠 **QUARTERBACK SNEAK**—A play where the quarterback keeps the ball and tries to "sneak" past the defensive line.

🧠 **ROLE PLAYERS**—People who are asked to do specific things when they are in a game.

🧠 **ROOKIE**—A player in his first year.

🧠 **SACKED**—Tackled the quarterback behind the line of scrimmage.

🧠 **SPECIAL TEAMS**—The groups of players who take the field for punts, kickoffs, field goals, and extra points.

🧠 **SUPER BOWL**—The championship of the NFL, played between the winners of the National Football Conference and American Football Conference.

🧠 *TRAITS*—Qualities that make someone stand out.

OVERTIME

TEAM SPIRIT introduces a great way to stay up to date with your team! Visit our **OVERTIME** link and get connected to the latest and greatest updates. **OVERTIME** serves as a young reader's ticket to an exclusive web page—with more stories, fun facts, team records, and photos of the Seahawks. Content is updated during and after each season. The **OVERTIME** feature also enables readers to send comments and letters to the author! Log onto:

www.norwoodhousepress.com/library.aspx

and click on the tab: **TEAM SPIRIT** to access **OVERTIME**.

Read all the books in the series to learn more about professional sports. For a complete listing of the baseball, basketball, football, and hockey teams in the **TEAM SPIRIT** series, visit our website at:

www.norwoodhousepress.com/library.aspx

On the Road

SEATTLE SEAHAWKS
800 Occidental Avenue South
Seattle, Washington 98134
888-635-4295
www.seahawks.com

THE PRO FOOTBALL HALL OF FAME
2121 George Halas Drive NW
Canton, Ohio 44708
330-456-8207
www.profootballhof.com

On the Bookshelf

To learn more about the sport of football, look for these books at your library or bookstore:

* Frederick, Shane. *The Best of Everything Football Book.* North Mankato, Minnesota: Capstone Press, 2011.

* Jacobs, Greg. *The Everything Kids' Football Book: The All-Time Greats, Legendary Teams, Today's Superstars—And Tips on Playing Like a Pro.* Avon, Massachusetts: Adams Media Corporation, 2010.

* Editors of *Sports Illustrated for Kids. 1st and 10: Top 10 Lists of Everything in Football.* New York, New York: Sports Illustrated Books, 2011.

Index

PAGE NUMBERS IN **BOLD** REFER TO ILLUSTRATIONS.

About the Author

MARK STEWART has written more than 50 books on football and over 150 sports books for kids. He grew up in New York City during the 1960s rooting for the Giants and Jets, and was lucky enough to meet players from both teams. Mark comes from a family of writers. His grandfather was Sunday Editor of *The New York Times,* and his mother was Articles Editor of *Ladies' Home Journal* and *McCall's*. Mark has profiled hundreds of athletes over the past 25 years. He has also written several books about his native New York and New Jersey, his home today. Mark is a graduate of Duke University, with a degree in history. He lives and works in a home overlooking Sandy Hook, New Jersey. You can contact Mark through the Norwood House Press website.

ML

9-15